The Art of Small Talk

Because Dating's Not a Science—It's an Art

Hayley DiMarco
and Michael DiMarco

Revell
Grand Rapids, Michigan

© 2007 by Hungry Planet

Published by Fleming H. Revell
a division of Baker Publishing Group
P.O. Box 6287, Grand Rapids, MI 49516-6287
www.revellbooks.com

Printed in the United States of America

Library of Congress Cataloging-in-Publication Data is on file
at the Library of Congress, Washington, D.C.

ISBN 10: 0-8007-3145-X
ISBN 978-0-8007-3145-8

Published in association with Yates & Yates, LLP, Literary Agents,
Orange, California.

The Art of Small Talk

THE
MARRIABLE
GALLERY

talk

# of Modern
Small Talk
Art

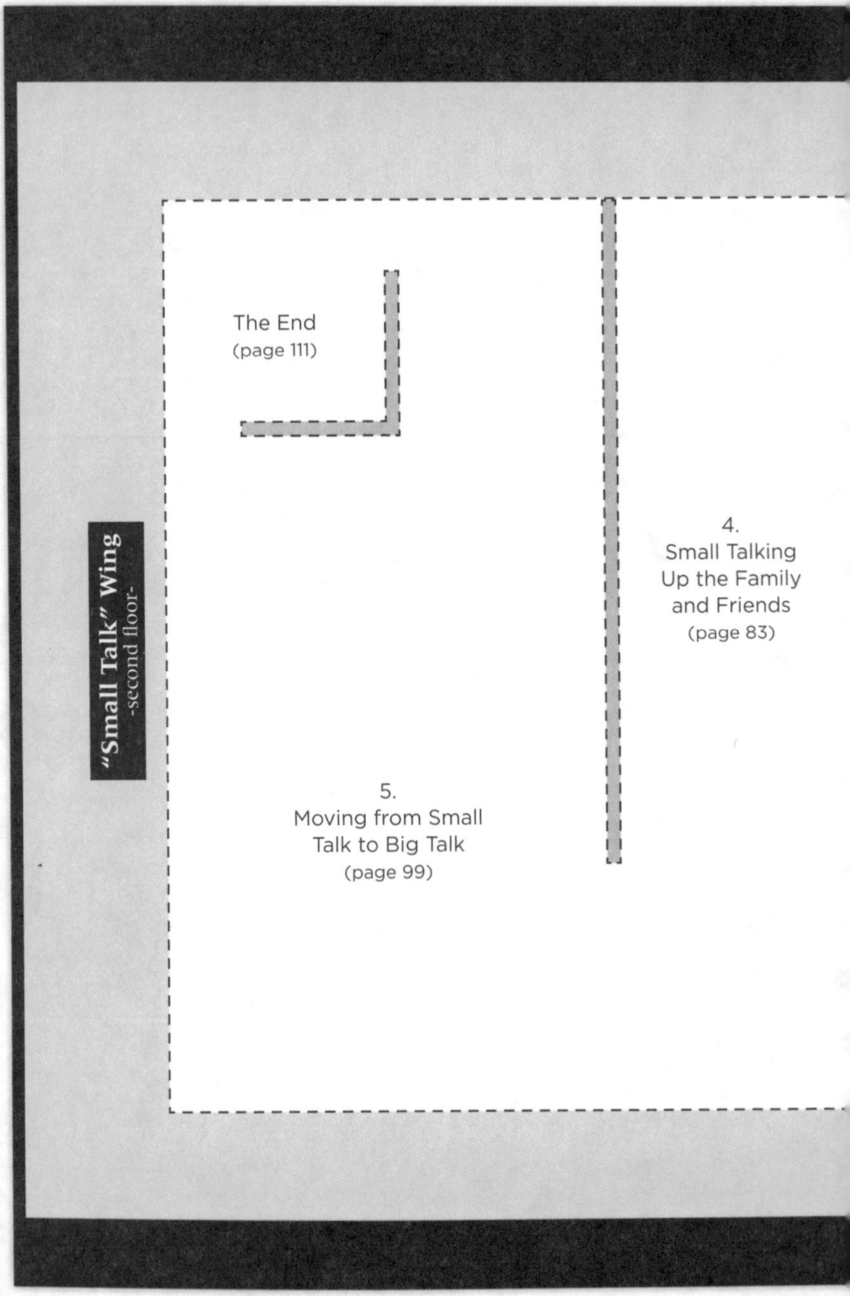
"Small Talk" Wing
-second floor-
The End
(page 111)
4.
Small Talking
Up the Family
and Friends
(page 83)
5.
Moving from Small
Talk to Big Talk
(page 99)

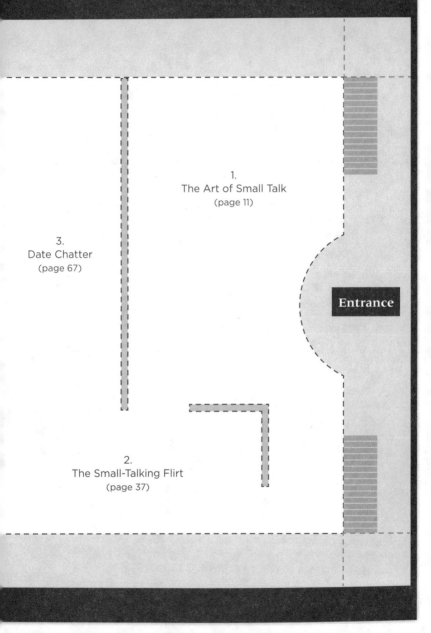

Entrance

small talk:

light, informal conversation
for social occasions

also known as . . .

chitchat

gabfest

gab

tittle-tattle

gossip

chin-wagging

chin-wag

causerie

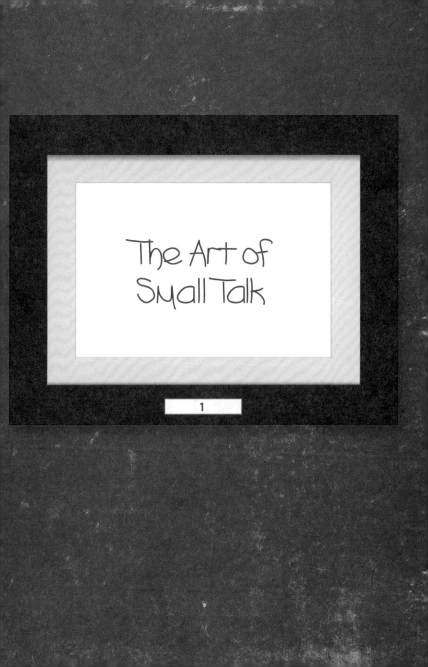

The Art of Small Talk

1

To approach the stranger is to invite the unexpected, release a new force, let the genie out of the bottle. It is to start a new train of events that is beyond your control.

—T. S. Eliot

Have you ever felt the agony of silence? You're sitting next to someone you think you really like. You search and claw and grasp at thoughts in your head, hoping that one of them will make its way out of your mouth and into the air. But nothing. Silence. You can't think of one single thing to say, and you see a potential relationship slipping silently out of your hands. Oh, the agony! Many a potential relationship has been thwarted by this silent killer. But have no fear. There is hope. If you aren't the best at shooting the breeze, chatting people up, or generating that stuff called small talk, it doesn't have to be that way forever. You can learn the Art of Small Talk, and you can turn your dating and social life around.

If you've never mastered the Art of Small Talk, you might need to better understand its purpose. Small talk is that amazing thing that allows you to slowly and comfortably get to know another person. It helps you keep a healthy pace in the relationship and gives you plenty of opportunities to cut and run from something that isn't going where you want it to go. Small talk gives you the power to make wise decisions instead of dysfunctional ones. If you aren't looking for just a one-night stand but want the real thing, then small talk is a must. Imagine an online ad that says, "Meet singles interested in NO small talk!" Sound dreamy? Well, it does for some—those interested in something *other* than getting to know a complete stranger before diving into, shall we say, "romance." But if you aren't willing to skip the "getting to know you" part, then you have to face it: Small talk is a must.

We rabbits have never gone in for much small talk.

You might be saying, "But why does it have to be 'small' talk? Why can't we talk about really meaningful things like our faith or political passions?" And to that we say, "Slooww the boat

13

Not *that* slow!

down, Skipper!" It would be great if you could just jump right into an already healthy, communicative, caring, and understanding relationship on the first or second date. But that ain't happening. It takes time to develop that kind of relationship, and until that time comes, small talk is the foundation that has to be laid. So if you've avoided small talk because it just seems so, well, uh, *small*, wake up! Small talk should actually be called "really big deal talk," because it is crucial to creating—and growing—deep and important relationships.

Small Talk 101

The Art of Small Talk: the ability to create safe, comfortable, fun, and easy-flowing conversation with a complete stranger in hopes of making them less of a stranger very soon.

Small talk is essentially conversation that is light, easy, and even funny and isn't likely to lead to an all-out verbal battle with your "new friend." Because you don't know this person too well, it's safe to say that you don't know their hot buttons. You don't know the topics that might send them through the roof or into a pool of tears. For example, if you sit down on a first date and start to talk to Kelsey about your deep-seated belief that the death penalty is the only answer to stopping rampant crime, it might put a damper on the evening when she tells you how her father was put to death by lethal injection last September before the DNA evidence exonerated him in October. Ouch! If we had a nickel for every time we've heard that one! Many a dating disaster can be attributed to one or both parties having a complete misunderstanding of the Art of Small Talk.

So before we get started, let's have a look at a few personality types who might have failed their small talk midterm but don't want to fail the final exam.

The Nice Guy

Wise men talk because they have something to say; fools, because they have to say something.

—Plato

In *Marriable: Taking the Desperate Out of Dating*, we said that "nice guys finish last." And as many a nice guy can attest, that is often the case, at least when it comes to women. You'll have to look at *Marriable* to learn all the reasons that's the case, but let's look at this one glaring problem: The nice guy has taken a magic marker to the Art of Small Talk and covered over all the fine lines and beautiful hues in favor of telling all and being "emotionally open." Nice guys have this mixed-up notion that women really want them to be as emotional as a girl. They think women want them to share their deepest feel-

A non-magic marker. The magic one disappeared on us.

ings, cry at sad movies, express their deepest longings, and take the lead in moving the relationship along emotionally. And so to them small talk seems like picking a daisy when filling the room with roses would work so much better! Nice guys tend to take a first or second date as an opportunity to impress upon a woman how much they care. So they say things like, "I've never felt so much so fast for someone," or "I really can't wait to start having kids." Essentially, they overshare. More often than not, this traditionally female trait of being emotionally giddy and transparent backfires for the nice guy because the girl just feels smothered. After all, it isn't only men who like a bit of mystery. The bad boy that you hear so many women pining for isn't running off at the mouth emotionally, sharing too much, too soon. Nope, chances are he has conquered the Art of Small Talk—oh-so-very-small talk. We're not saying that being the bad boy should be your goal, but his inability to open up is a good study in how not oversharing can be a real turn-on to the opposite sex.

Nice guys, you need to understand that in the beginning of a relationship, small talk has much more power than emotional bloodletting. Small talk will allow you to seem mysterious and manly while at the same time allowing you to learn more about the object of your affections, not to

17

mention guard your heart. In fact, it allows you to guard your date's heart as well, and who doesn't love the hero? Small talk allows the woman to put out her emotional feelers to decide if you are worth spending more time with before she divulges her inner self to you. If you've read *Marriable*, you've heard it all before: Women are much more comfortable keeping the emotional pace of the relationship than allowing the guy to take control of the feelings and thus decide how deep they are going how fast. In the early stages of a relationship, the overly emotional and sharing man is a real turn-off to most women.

For you, making small talk might be a big change, but if you keep doing what you're doing, you're gonna keep getting what you're getting. And how's that working for you?

*If talking were aerobic, I'd be the thinnest
person in the world.*

—Carrie Fisher

Women have a tendency to talk. And that's
not a slam, it's just a fact. Women bond by talking. No big deal. But when it comes to guys,
that's not the case. Guys don't bond when words
are spoken. They don't feel more for you because they've heard more about you. In fact, it's
just the opposite. The truth is that for men, a
woman of mystery is always a much more cov-
eted woman than one who wears her emotional
life on her sleeve. If you're an active talker, then
maybe "not too much information" needs to be
your new mantra. TMI can send a guy running
as fast as watercolor paint in a rainstorm.

Bonding won't
happen if you
use too much
"glue".

Like we said in *Marriable*, guys love a challenge, and chasing a girl who shares TMI is like
playing hide-and-seek with someone who hides
in the middle of the room with their eyes closed
and says, "Come find me!" Boring! So if you

19

want to change your luck with men, you might want to check out your talk-o-meter. If you are registering high and finding that you are using up all your 20,000 words a day on your date, you might want to consider the "less is more" approach to small talk.

The TMI Guy

The best way to be boring is to leave nothing out.

—Voltaire

Just a minor disclaimer that at first might seem like a contradiction to what we just said, but bear with us: Men, women love to talk. That's how they bond, and because of that, if you don't shut up and listen to her, she's going to think you aren't interested. Say a guy goes on a date with a girl. All night he won't shut up. She tries to get a word in here and there but doesn't get to talk too much about herself. Girl goes home, calls up her best friend, and says, "What a total waste! I didn't get to say a word. All he did was talk about himself! Guess he's just not interested in me." If a girl can't talk about herself, she won't feel like she's bonded to you in any way. So even though we just told women to shut up a little and not share TMI, we know she has to share a decent amount of information or she'll wilt on the vine. So make sure that you aren't doing the majority of the talking if you're a guy. The key to small talk with a woman is keeping some of the focus on her. We'll get to that soon enough. Just remember, girls bond by talking, so give her a break and share the conversation 50–50 or, preferably, 60–40 (with the girl getting 60). She'll love you for it.

Small Talk = 50–50?

He who refuses to do arithmetic is doomed to talk nonsense.
—John McCarthy

When it comes to conversation, especially early on, a good rule of thumb is 50–50. That allows the girl to get her bonding on and the guy not to have to drown in a sea of oversharing (or vice versa, as sometimes the case may be). A 50–50 split means that both of you are pulling your weight and neither person is hogging the word count. Think of it like a beautiful dance or a great game of one-on-one b-ball. Conversation easily flows back and forth, with each person taking their turn, one at a time, and creating an enjoyable experience. If one person hogs the ball, the game can be a disaster. Small talk is no different; it requires a continual give and take—no hogging.

But the truth is, if you're a guy who tends to overshare, 50–50 is 1 percent away from you oversharing. And since your muscle memory is built up toward that end, we heartily recommend a 60–40 rule for small talk (and big talk), with the girl getting the 60. And while we told girls not to run off at the mouth, we fully expect the girl to use more words on a date than the guy. Hey, scientific studies put it at three words from a woman to every one word that exits a man's mouth!

Please, don't share everything.

Mastering the art of turn-taking is managing your listening skills. Try thinking of yourself as a listener using these five "soler" power steps to attentive listening:

S quarely face the person

O pen your posture

L ean toward the sender

E ye contact maintained

R elax while listening

22

Using these nonverbal cues will help you relax, not feel the need to interrupt, and at the same time give your date your undivided attention. Who wouldn't love that?

Once you master the 60–40 rule, you can start to manage the conversation to ensure an even playing field. If you realize you've been talking way more than the other person, it's time to pass the ball. Do what you can to quickly turn the conversation back to their side of the court. Ask them a question that can't be answered with yes or no. Get them to talking and then—here's the key—shut up and listen! If two people are good at throwing it back and forth, the game is on and the date should be a success. Even if you end up having no physical chemistry, you can have some stimulating conversation or at the very least a good practice run at the Art of Small Talk.

Small Talking Preparation

Before you master the Art of Small Talk, you're going to need some practice time. Artists aren't born painting masterpieces; they spend time honing and growing their talent, and with practice they get to a place where they can be called true artists. The same is true for the Art of Small Talk. You aren't necessarily born being good at it, but over time and with practice you can become a true master.

Talk to Familiar Strangers

At the bottom of enmity between strangers lies indifference.

—Søren Kierkegaard

The perfect place for you to start your small talk practice is with people you aren't so intimidated by. In other words, people you aren't going to date. A huge group of the opposite sex is out there, and they are perfect blank canvases for your first attempt at becoming a small talk artiste! These are people who you are around every day but have no real intimate knowledge of or relationship with. They are people in the service industry. When you think about it, they're perfect because they spend all day talking to people, so they're usually good at small talk, and they're safe because they aren't just some stranger on the subway who might follow you home because you took an interest in them. The kinds of people we're talking about are the checkout clerk, cab driver, receptionist, waiter, flight attendant, hostess, grocery store cashier, and so on. We find that most of them love to chat, and if they don't, well, then the real challenge begins because it gives you a great chance to learn to draw people out. Even the somber-faced, silent checkout clerk can light up when you notice they are more than fingers punching buttons. It's a win-win situation when you practice small talk on strangers because small talk can make a person feel noticed. Think about how many people just robotically go through their day, never being looked in the eye by any of the hundreds of people they come into contact with. Day in and day out, we too often completely ignore the very people who are working so hard to serve us or even who just happen to cross our paths. Practicing small

Why, thank you. I think you have nice teeth too.

talk is a great way to care for those people as you work on your own skills.

And besides, you never know the kind of people small talk can allow you to meet and care for. You might even get other people around you involved in conversation when you open up your eyes and mouth and notice the value of people around you. And who knows, maybe a cutie somewhere nearby will hear something interesting and join in on your interesting small talk fest. Many a friendship has been started by just such casual conversations in mundane places like the grocery store or bus stand. And this practice comes in handy when you start dating because your date will see in you a person who naturally engages people who most see as insignificant to their day. So practice, practice. Talk to those people you see every day. Care about what they say. Learn to interact and to find ways of using small talk to make the world a better place.

Small Talk = Confidence

Confidence is a really attractive character trait. People are attracted to and interested in people with confidence. But if you aren't feeling too confident, you can still look confident by changing one little thing—how you interact with familiar strangers. Nothing exudes confidence more than someone who cares enough to talk to the people around them. The Art of Small Talk can really impress the one you have your eye on.

27

Talk without effort is nothing.
—Maria W. Stewart

The next thing you have to master in small talk is subject matter or topics. What kind of stuff are you going to gab about? The more you do your research, the more colors you have for your small talk palette. So here's what to do: Read, watch, and listen to anything you can get your hands on. Each magazine article you read, movie you see, and song or talk show you listen to gives you great inspiration for small talk. Even what seems like a completely weird subject can still become a very interesting subject for small talk.

If you're not a reader, there are plenty of other media options for you. Talk radio is ripe with small talk tidbits. Be careful, though, because a lot of talk radio covers subjects that might get your date's guard up. Remember, avoid politics, religion, and other inflammatory topics on a first or second meeting.

Besides gleaning small talk topics through reading and listening, you can also *do* things that are small talk worthy. Cultural activities like theater, music, sports, and poetry will also up the possibilities for topics. So dive into life. You'll get a great start on the Art of Small Talk and maybe even be entertained in the process.

Here are some great starters for your next small talk conversation.

These might require some preparation (i.e., research). So get to reading!

- An upcoming concert or movie
- A weird skill you learned something about last week
- Your hobby or their hobby
- Some little known trivia about where you're going on your date
- The latest plans for a new area of development in the city
- A strange invention that you saw on TV

Did You Know?

Here are some interesting facts that might help you along with the Art of Small Talk. Being armed with this kind of stuff can make you a very interesting person to be with, or at least a quirky one. (Note: Use these sparingly. Don't run down the list with your date unless the topic of conversation is trivia geeks. These work best if they actually have something to do with where you are or what you're talking about.)

- If a statue of a person on a horse has both front legs of the horse in the air, the person died in battle. If the horse has one front leg in the air, the person died as a result of wounds received in battle. If the horse has all four legs on the ground, the person died of natural causes.
- No word in the English language completely rhymes with *month*, *orange*, *silver*, or *purple*.
- Clans of long ago that wanted to get rid of their unwanted people without killing them used to burn their houses down—hence the expression "to get fired." Donald Trump, the pyromaniac. Who knew?

- There are two credit cards for every person in the United States.
- Only two people signed the Declaration of Independence on July 4, 1776: John Hancock and Charles Thomson. Most of the rest signed on August 2, but the last signature wasn't added until five years later.
- The shortest complete sentence in the English language is "I am."
- The term "the whole nine yards" came from World War II fighter pilots in the South Pacific. The .50-caliber machine gun ammo belts measured exactly twenty-seven feet long before being loaded into the fuselage of the plane. If a pilot fired all his ammo at a target, it got "the whole nine yards."
- The most common name in the world is Mohammed.
- The glue on Israeli postage stamps is certified kosher.

→

- Mel Blanc (the voice of Bugs Bunny) was allergic to carrots.
- Until 1965, driving was done on the left-hand side of roads in Sweden. The conversion to the right-hand side was done on a weekday at 5:00 p.m. All traffic stopped as people switched sides. This time and day were chosen to prevent accidents from happening because drivers would have gotten up in the morning and been too sleepy to realize that *this* was the day of the changeover.
- The very first bomb dropped by the Allies on Berlin during World War II killed the only elephant in the Berlin Zoo.
- More people are killed annually by donkeys than die in air crashes.
- The phrase "It's all fun and games until someone loses an eye" is from ancient Rome. The only rule during wrestling matches was "no eye gouging." Everything else was allowed. The only

way to be disqualified was to poke someone's eye out.
- A "jiffy" is an actual unit of time, measuring one one-hundredth of a second.
- The average person falls asleep in seven minutes.
- Hershey's Kisses are called that because the machine that makes them looks like it's kissing the conveyor belt.
- Money isn't made out of paper; it's made out of cotton.
- Every time you lick a stamp, you're consuming one tenth of a calorie.
- The phrase "rule of thumb" is derived from an old English law that stated that a man couldn't beat his wife with anything wider than his thumb.
- An ostrich's eye is bigger than its brain.
- The longest recorded flight of a chicken is thirteen seconds.

Risk It

If you're willing to take a few risks, you can really get some great ammo for small talk by doing new things. Try a new restaurant everyone's been talking about. Take dance lessons or go to a photography class. It's like this: The more you grow yourself mentally and emotionally, the better you can get at small talk. The more things you're doing, the more stuff you have to talk about.

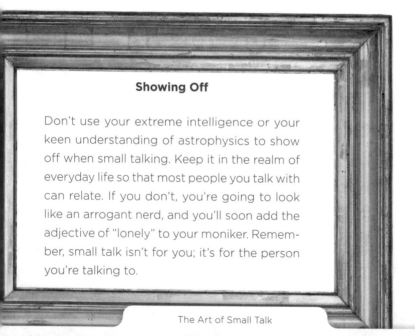

Showing Off

Don't use your extreme intelligence or your keen understanding of astrophysics to show off when small talking. Keep it in the realm of everyday life so that most people you talk with can relate. If you don't, you're going to look like an arrogant nerd, and you'll soon add the adjective of "lonely" to your moniker. Remember, small talk isn't for you; it's for the person you're talking to.

The most difficult thing for people to say in twenty-five words or less is good-bye.

—Anonymous

Before we leave the Art of Small Talk, we need to mention an often overlooked tool of the small talker: the exit. Sometimes you can end up with a really chatty small talk partner who just wants your talk to be anything but small. They'll chat your ear off if you let them, and if they aren't someone you are interested in, you'll need a line or two in your back pocket to help you gracefully walk away from the conversation. Spend some time thinking of something clever to say, or just remember one or two of these lines:

"Thanks for the chat, but I should make my rounds and talk to some other people."

"It was nice chatting with you. Hope you have a great day!"

"Well, I'd better go check on my five kids I left locked in the car."

The Small-Talking Flirt

2

God made mud, *God* made dirt, *God* made boys so girls could flirt.

—Anonymous

For a lot of guys, asking a woman out can be treacherous. And the fear of rejection can be crippling. (If that sounds like you or someone you know, then check out another *Marriable* book of ours called *The Art of Rejection*.) But there is an answer to not knowing whether she'll smile and say yes as she bats her eyes or look at you with pity for even supposing that she was in your league. That answer is flirting. Flirting, in most cases, is really just small talk with a specific purpose—helping someone to figure out that you like them. Flirting isn't just fun; it's good for you! Just think of it: No more wondering whether or not she'll laugh at you. No more chasing men, asking for their phone numbers and feeling like *you* have to do all the work. Flirting gives you insight into the feelings of the other person without ever coming out and saying, "So, do you like me?" We tend to

The Small-Talking Flirt

flirt subconsciously. When we like someone, flirtatious comments just well up inside most of us, and we have to let them out. If the other person responds in kind, then the small talk can be stimulating. But flirting small talk can also be a learned art, one that you spend some time and effort polishing. If you want to be more available to the people around you who interest you and find out if something could happen between you, then get to work on your flirting small talk.

Flirting with Intent

In *Marriable* we talked a lot about the nonverbal flirting cues we give to people, but in this book we want to talk more about the verbal sparring involved in flirting. First of all, understand that small talk of any kind can often be interpreted as flirting, so be careful about the things you say if you aren't in any way hoping to find chemistry with another person. Choosing words wisely is an important skill in the Art of Small Talk. When

Choosing wisely is important for more than just small talk.

it comes to flirting, small talk is really ramped up a notch. The things we say have an undercurrent of interest beneath them. Double meanings abound when small talk turns to flirting. So just make sure that when you start flirting with someone, your intent is to get their interest and to take the relationship into the dating realm or beyond. Flirting for the fun of it can end up hurting people's feelings and even putting you in harm's way. So don't lead people on with flirting. Use it as a tool to express your feelings of attraction in a non-aggressive, playful way.

Places *to* Flirt

- Parties
- Weddings
- Grocery stores
- Restaurants
- Classes
- Standing in line

Places *Not* to Flirt

- Funerals
- Your boss's office
- Business meetings
- In court
- Church services

Flirting Wisely

Since flirting small talk is so much more purposeful than most forms of small talk, it's important to understand your *Marriable* worth. We went into this in depth in *Marriable*, so we won't belabor the point. But suffice it to say that if you're a '76 Volkswagen Beetle, you shouldn't be going after a 2006 Ferrari. Flirting success generally requires that you flirt with someone who is roughly as attractive as you are. Sure, you can shoot for the stars and try to flirt with the mega-hottie in the black turtleneck, but don't be surprised when they give you a pity laugh and strike up a conversation with someone next to them.

Being honest with yourself about your *Marriable* worth can be really difficult for both sexes. In general, women tend to underestimate themselves, thinking that they're just too fat or having a bad hair day. They are unlikely to think too highly of themselves, while men are just the op- posite. Men tend not to obsess about things like weight, hair, skin texture, and so on. And because of that fact, they don't mark themselves down for areas in which they might just be lacking, so they can tend to overestimate their true *Marriable* worth. All this to say that it's very important to have a realistic view of yourself before diving into the Art of Small Talk Flirting.

According to the Social Issues Research Center, although more men are overweight, women are ten times more likely to dislike their shape and have a distorted body image. In fact, 80 percent of women think they're too fat. Because women are much more critical of their appearance than men, they are much less likely to admire what they see in the mirror. In other words, they don't know their own *Marriable* worth.

Source: "Mirror, Mirror: A Summary of Research Findings on Body Image," Kate Fox, Social Issues Research Center, 1997, http://www.sirc.org/publik/mirror.html

Verbal Sparring: The Art of Flirting

Researchers say that when you first meet someone, their first impression of you is based 55 percent on your appearance and body language, 38 percent on your style of speaking, and only 7 percent on what you actually say. Okay, so it's over half about how you look. But 45 percent of it is about what you say and how you say it. Looks aren't everything. Small talk can make or break the deal. Have you ever seen a person who was really attractive—until they opened their mouth? Suddenly all those dashing good looks just became completely unimportant because they talk like a donkey! Since you can't spend your entire life with your mouth shut, why not work on the Art of Small Talk so you can have a better chance of seeing a smile instead of the back of their head?

Tone Deaf?

"Bueller? Bueller?" drones the voice of actor Ben Stein. It's a classic moment in the film *Ferris Bueller's Day Off*. Can you imagine meeting someone who was attractive but when they spoke said everything in monotone? You'd either want to say, "Here!" or turn tail and run. Either

44

way, you'd probably lose interest as soon as they opened their mouth. Tone and delivery are often-overlooked aspects of small talk. It's important not only *what* you say but also *how* you say it. Tone, volume, speed, and pitch can all have as much to do with what you communicate as the words you are using. The character of Joey Tribbiani from *Friends* offers a classic example of using tone, speed, and pitch to convey a meaning other than the words being used. "How *you* doin'?" suddenly doesn't sound like a simple question about the state of your emotions but sounds more like a tawdry pickup line from a sex-crazed starving actor. Try this trick out yourself. Say the word "hi" in a bunch of different ways and see how many meanings you can give this simple greeting.

Hi.
(Whoa, . . . check out his tone of voice on that.)

Sometimes your tone and delivery can even completely change words to the opposite of their true meaning. Try saying "I love you" but making it sound like you are lying and you really mean you hate the person. Or like you're being sarcastic and you don't actually love them, but you are actually mad at them. The *way* you say

45

something has just become more important than *what* you say!

Tone and delivery style can also affect the appearance of confidence. A confident person, or at least someone who can fake it really well, has a confident way of delivering their words. If you have a weak delivery or an inability to sound confident, then you might need to do some work. In the video game The Sims, you can send your Sims to the mirror to practice their charisma. The longer they spend in front of the mirror talking, the more charisma points they get. It might seem kind of stupid, but it works. Just think, you can be like thousands of actors who spend hours in front of the mirror practicing their lines so they can win the hearts of the American public.

Speaking of great delivery.

Witty Small Talk

See a hottie next to you but have no clue what to say to a complete stranger? Here are a few conversation starters to get the ball rolling. If the stranger feels the same attraction and they aren't too clueless or shy, they'll start the banter back to you.

To person on computer in coffee shop: "How do you like your laptop? I'm thinking of getting one like it."

To person reading the paper: "Are you through with the entertainment section of your paper?" Then ask them if they've seen such and such a movie and what they thought of it.

In line ordering food: "I'm torn. What do you think sounds better, _____ or _____?"

In a bookstore: "Do you know the name of the new novel by _____?"

At the gym: "Hey, can you show me how to use this machine?" (Use this only if you're a girl!) Or "Where did you get those shoes? Are they good for running?"

At the park: "Would you mind getting in this picture with me? I'm sending it to a friend and I want them to stop nagging me to get a girl/boyfriend."

Small Talk Flirting Etiquette

Small talk flirting etiquette can save you a lot of issues with "foot-in-mouth" disease. When it comes to small talk flirting, it's important that you know the rules of engagement before diving in. This might be a little more difficult for guys than girls, because girls are so well versed in the business of talking. But that doesn't mean men can't be great small talkers. So here are a few things to think about before you flirt with flirting.

Studies have shown that women tend to be more skilled at informal social conversation than men, both because they are naturally more socially sensitive and because they have better verbal and communication skills.

Don't Spend All Your Time Talking about Yourself

Don't talk about what you have done or what you are going to do.

—Thomas Jefferson

"Recent research has revealed only one significant difference between male and female gossip: men spend much more time talking about themselves. Of the total time devoted to conversation about social relationships, men spend two thirds talking about their own relationships, while women only talk about themselves one third of the time."

I think I look quite manly with my Chia-hippo look.

Source: "Evolution, Alienation, and Gossip,"
Kate Fox, Social Issues Research Center, 2001,
http://www.sirc.org/publik/gossip.shtml

In order for people to get to know you, you have to talk about yourself, but balance is key. Too much talking about yourself is an instant turn-off. But so is not *ever* talking about yourself at all. If you are going to err, err on the side of not talking enough about yourself. It will add a little mystery. Going the other way won't do a thing but end the conversation faster. We won't belabor this point too much; suffice it to say that a little mystery goes a long way. So don't dump the inner you onto someone when small talk is the best tool for the job.

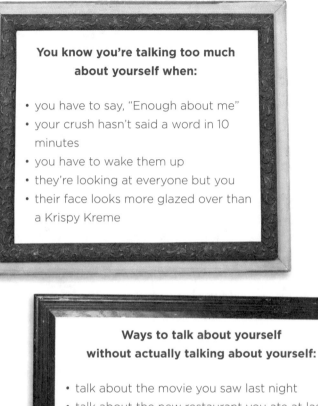

You know you're talking too much about yourself when:

- you have to say, "Enough about me"
- your crush hasn't said a word in 10 minutes
- you have to wake them up
- they're looking at everyone but you
- their face looks more glazed over than a Krispy Kreme

Ways to talk about yourself without actually talking about yourself:

- talk about the movie you saw last night
- talk about the new restaurant you ate at last week
- talk about the latest trend you're interested in
- avoid using the word *I* or *my* more than a couple of times; stick to words like *they*, *some people*, *have you heard*, etc.

51

What is the very first thing that comes out of your mouth when you meet someone who rotates your radials? You're feeling the fire, so do you start with something hot and clever, like "Are you from Tennessee? Because you're the only ten I see!"? Or do you go for the more mundane, "Nice weather we're having, huh?" It makes a huge difference which way you go on the first meet. You might think that because you're interested in the person and you want them to understand that you're flirting, you oughta start with something witty and flirtatious. But the exact opposite is true most of the time. Starting off the conversation with something obviously flirtatious can be the death knell for a relationship. It's a shock to the system to dive right in to flirting that quickly. It's like jumping into a cold pool after just getting out of the Jacuzzi. And it's a dangerous move. You haven't even established yet if they are interested or not. So diving right in with the flirting is really presumptuous and can make the person feel freaked out—besides the fact that it just plain makes you sound desperate. Most women assume that when a guy uses a pickup line (i.e., flirtatious comment) as the first words out of his mouth, he is just trolling one woman after another until he finds one who's naive enough to believe him. Now, if you're Brad Pitt or something and she's already been drooling over you, the corny pickup line might work, but chances are you aren't Mr. Pitt, so your best bet is to avoid the pickup line.

The thing to remember is that although the first contact is the beginning of flirting, it shouldn't sound flirtatious. A good opening line should be casually conversational and maybe even slightly humorous. In other words, it should give the person the option either to smile and say something back to you that will indicate that they want to keep talking or to be cold and standoffish so you get the picture and leave them alone. When that happens, some people get all uptight and angry about how rude the person was. But what you should be doing is thanking them for not wasting your time by leading you on. How people respond to your opening line should be an indicator of how much attraction they are feeling. So if you keep the opening statement to a simple, casual question that can be answered with a yes or no, you'll save yourself a lot of time and energy.

Avoid direct questions that make them have to respond in detail. Instead, make a statement that they can either comment on or ignore.

Good Opening Lines—Make a statement and raise your voice at the end to make it a pseudo-question, especially if the answer is obvious. That way they have the option of grunting or answering (i.e., making the next move or slamming the door).

- "I wonder if it could be any louder in here."
- "If it rains any more, we're going to have to call a canoe instead of a taxi."

Bad Opening Lines—Never use the opening line to show how cheesy or desperate you are. A little humor isn't bad, but over the top sends yellow and red flags a-flying.

- "When do you have to get back to heaven?"
- "Are your legs tired? Because you've been running through my mind since you walked in."

The Small-Talking Flirt

Take Turns

One unbreakable rule of small talk is *take turns*! That's why they call it *small* talk and not oh-my-gosh-could-you-ever-shut-up talk. You have to take turns when it comes to getting to know someone. If all you ever do is talk about yourself or hog the conversation, then they'll think you're either totally self-obsessed or just plain not interested in them. That means that you have to check the conversation. Make sure that when there is a significant pause, you fill it in, but also that you add enough significant pauses of your own so they can jump in. If they seem hesitant to talk, then you can always ask them questions they can't answer with yes or no to help them along. But whatever you do, don't mess up on the 50–50 rule. Keep it even.

Asking Questions—The best questions to ask start with *who*, *what*, *where*, *when*, *why*, or *how*. That way the other person has to give you more than a one-word answer. Think like a reporter and you'll give great small talk.

"One study found that the length of the average pause during speech was 0.807 seconds, while the average pause between speakers was shorter, only 0.764 seconds."

Source: "SIRC Guide to Flirting," Kate Fox, Social Issues Research Center, n.d., http://www.sirc.org/publik/flirt.html

The Small-Talking Flirt

Listen

If the person you are talking to doesn't appear to be listening, be patient. It may simply be that he has a small piece of fluff in his ear.

—Winnie the Pooh

Asking questions leads us to listening. Small talk isn't only about talking; it's just as much about listening. Another person can really tell if you are sincere or not by how well you listen. And no, you can't listen and watch the TV at the same time. Pay attention to who's talking, and act interested. Of course, this involves a lot of nonverbal feedback, which we touched on in *Marriable*, but you know the drill. Nod, smile, say things like "Oh, wow," "Yep," "Uh-huh," and "How interesting." Of course, all that can be faked. But the faking soon becomes apparent when you can't or don't add anything more to the topic. It's essential to add something more to the conversation than just verbal and nonverbal "cues." You will be tons more *Marriable* to someone if you can actually contribute to the conversation on their topic of choice. You don't have to be an expert on what they are saying, but you can remember something in your life that ties into what they are talking about or ask them questions that will further the exploration of their topic. Small talk gets really fun when the banter goes back and forth.

Fake it till you make it. It might seem unnatural at first, this small talk stuff, and you might feel like a fraud because you just read it in a book and started doing it. But just like love isn't purely an emotion, it's an action, so is small talk. Sometimes you have to force yourself to practice and to pursue the Art of Small Talk. But after a while it becomes second nature and part of your character. So don't worry about feeling like you're faking or playing games. It's just a feeling, and it will pass.

*Don't use words too big for the subject. Don't say "infinitely"
when you mean "very"; otherwise you'll have no word left
when you want to talk about something really infinite.*

—C. S. Lewis

When it comes to conversing with someone you just met or want to get to know better, you need to remember a few rules of good small talk. This time of small talk is a time to shine. It's not a time to show off your extreme side. Therefore, avoid the following: negativity, boredom, arrogance, being too serious, fanaticism, too much enthusiasm, slow talking, close talking, fast talking, silence, teaching talk, talking down . . . you getting the picture? Stay away from racy, sexy, or just plain stupid jokes. Avoid talking about aeronautical engineering, unless you're both attending space camp. Basically, try to be someone who is smooth around the edges. Save your wild side for when you've gotten to know each other better. A good rule of thumb is to think about moderation. Too much of any one thing is too much. Too many compliments, ugh! Get a life! Too many questions? What is this, the third degree? Moderation is the key.

Small talk isn't talking about . . .

Once you've gotten beyond the initial introduction and opening line, small talk has to move forward. Here are some places *not* to go:

- the weather
- traffic
- your cat's fur balls
- a good B.M. or a lack thereof
- politics
- religion
- your ex
- your mom
- yourself

One more thing to be sure to add to your repertoire is the ability to get a little bit personal. When someone likes you—i.e., they're flirting with you—then they love to share and get back from you little personal tidbits that make the small talk a little more intimate. This helps both of you to come to an unstated agreement that this is more than a casual conversation and might just lead somewhere. The divulging doesn't have to be deep and shouldn't be too detailed, but dropping a few personal quips or stories can make for great flirting. It goes something like this: Your date shares that her dad used to take her fishing as a kid, and although she hates fishing, she loved spending that time with her dad. This is when you relate a childhood memory of casting a line and catching the hook in the shoulder of your jacket. The more you give each other personal information, the more aware you each become of the chemistry between you. It's like a green light, letting the other person know that you want to get closer to them. So don't use this lightly—personal info given to the wrong person could be a real tease!

As we said at the beginning of this chapter, the flirting we describe is intended for people who are using it with the intent of discovering whether there is chemistry between them. And if there is some kind of attraction, then dating is the desired ultimate outcome. If that's where you want to end up, then you'd better decide how you're going to get there. In *Marriable* we go into some of the details on chasing and pursuing, and we go even more in-depth in *The Art of the Chase*. It's quite normal today for a woman to ask a guy out, and we totally understand that. But the truth of the matter is that guys love a challenge. They love to chase; they love the adventure and intrigue of a woman who is a little harder to get than the one who is forcing her number on him. When a woman asks out a guy she's just met, you can bet that the guy, though he might be flattered, isn't thinking of her as "the one." What she's just told him by taking his role and being the aggressor is that she is a sexually aggressive woman or a woman who's going to be in charge. It's true; that's what guys think of the woman who takes the initiative. Because it's normally the male's role to do the asking and also the male's role to do the sexual pursuing, he translates your aggression in the asking department as a sign of your aggression in all aspects of the relationship, especially sex. The girls who men ultimately flip over seem to be the ones they had a harder time getting.

So men, let's talk about how to secure another chance to "get to know her" after your initial small talk conversation. You can't put all the effort into small talk flirting, find a real attraction, and then just shake hands and say, "It was nice talking to you." You have to have a plan and the courage to go after that plan. You want to see her again? Then ask her! Don't wait till she turns to walk away and hate yourself for not risking. Say something like, "I'd love to keep our conversation going, but I've got to run. Are you free for coffee this week?" If you are still afraid of the rejection thing, then pick up *The Art of Rejection* at your local bookstore. Rejection isn't all it's believed to be. There is a way around it, and when you've found a woman with chemistry, it's time to risk rejection and go on to bigger and better things.

Not to leave the women out. We know how hard it can be sometimes to find a guy who will

Do you know where you are headed with your flirting?

(Do you even know what this thing is? You can use this to find your direction when the batteries on your GPS unit die.)

The Small-Talking Flirt

take the initiative. They seem too fearful. And sometimes they are, but not of what you might think. They aren't always just afraid to ask you; they're afraid to offend you by being too forward. They're afraid you will feel like they are dangerous or creepy since you just met them. So you might have to help him out a bit if he's showing no signs of asking but all the signs of being interested. If that's the case, try nudging him a little. Have you ever seen a little kid tease another kid into chasing them? Think about how playful they look. Think about how they pick on the other kid just a little and then move away, hoping to show them that they want to be chased. Well, that's your job. Give them a little and then pull away, figuratively, in order to allow them to do the chasing. In other words, say something like, "You'll have to try the new coffee shop sometime," or "You play softball? I used to love watching my brother's team play. I wouldn't even mind playing if the team was co-ed." Get the picture? That's what you want him to do: get a picture of you two together at some point in the future. You don't have to

Some guys may even need a hair more than a gentle nudge.

The Small-Talking Flirt

come right out and ask him; in fact, you shouldn't, but you can tease him with the idea and then allow him to decide if he's man enough to chase after you. It's all a part of the Art of Small Talk Flirting: knowing how much information to give—and when to give it—in order to subtly share with your crush your feelings of attraction.

Date Chatter

3

Good *talk saves the food.*

—Anonymous

If you've made it through the first meeting and now you're on to an actual date, small talk can still be your friend. You can't dive into the first date any more than the first meeting as if you've known each other forever, sharing all of your deepest, darkest feelings. You have to start light, and that's why small talk works so well even on those initial "getting to know you" dates. Date chatter will determine whether there's going to be another chance for going deeper and deeper into each other's lives.

Something in Common

The royal road to a man's heart is to talk to him about the things he treasures most.

—Dale Carnegie

When it comes to small talk and wanting to connect with someone you are interested in, you really need to find things you have in common, things you both like to talk about. In fact, the more things you both like to talk about, the more smoothly the conversation will flow. Your goal in choosing topics is twofold: one, to find out if you have enough in common to make a relationship work, and two, to make the other person feel good about themselves, because when they feel good about themselves in your presence, they'll attribute that good feeling to the very fact that they're with you.

The first goal seems obvious. Some might say that opposites attract, but we say, they don't *stay* attracted! Having things in common really helps form the strongest bonds between people. Imagine spending the rest of your life with someone who didn't like anything that you liked. Or say they only liked a couple of things you liked—think of the distance that could create between you. Dating is your chance to find out what things you both like, agree with, are passionate about, etc., so that you can decide if it's worth your time pursuing the relationship.

The second goal of small talk, to make the other person feel good about themselves, may seem the most selfless. And maybe it is, but the truth behind it is that if you can make someone feel good about themselves while talking to you, that should make them want to see you more and more. Unless they just love being combative, people find the most pleasure in talking to someone who agrees with them or at least finds what they say insightful or interesting, not idiotic, argumentative, or boring. This part of the conversation isn't always completely in your control. You can't *make* people have the same ideas as you, so if you've found someone you just can't agree with, don't cry over spilled milk and try to make things work. Just chalk it up to good small talk practice and say your good-byes.

So how do you pick topics that might make you and your crush want to see each other more? Here are a few places to start:

The room—You are both in the same place, both seeing the same things and the same people; therefore, you are both *in the know*. So talking about interesting works of art on the wall or interesting people within your view can give you both a sense of agreement. Of course, if you disagree strongly about something in the room, it's best to drop the topic and move on to something a little more agreeable.

The city—You are also more than likely familiar with the city you are in. Talking about the feel of the city or the kinds of people who live there is a safe option for starting the small talk rolling. For example, if you are in NY, you can say, "I don't know what people are talking about. I think New Yorkers are super friendly!" Commenting on the city and its inhabitants is a great way to connect.

The food—If you're eating together, food can be inspiration for all kinds of small talk. Ask them what they like, if they've ever had it before, stuff like that. Also feel free to talk about your food and other places you've eaten that you've liked. Food seems to be a topic that most everyone can talk about.

Wow. Are you really going to eat that?

71

Be Yourself

Another important skill for the Art of Small Talk is the ability to be yourself. If you are trying overly hard to impress or be someone you are not, you will not succeed at small talk. People are most comfortable when the people they are with are comfortable with themselves. So no matter what, you have to feel free to be yourself. Now, that doesn't mean they get to see the whole enchilada. Feel free to hold some things back—this isn't your counselor's couch. We've already discussed TMI, so you get the picture. Be yourself, but that doesn't have to include sharing all of yourself.

Conversation Starters

If you've ever scanned your brain in vain searching for something, *anything*, to talk about with your date, then you'll appreciate these conversation starters. Don't just glance over them. Memorize them. Then when you get into your next small talking date, you won't have to squirm in silent horror at how little you can find in your brain.

72

Your Locale

At a restaurant: "So what do you think of the _____
_____ (food, decor, location)?"

At the movies: "Have you ever seen (name of another
movie)?"

At the movies: "What is your favorite film and why?"

At a coffeehouse: "So what's your favorite coffee
drink?"

Your Date

"Have you always lived here?"

"Do you have any brothers or sisters?"

"What do you like to do on your days off?"

"What's the best book you've ever read? Why?"

"What's the most annoying first date you've ever been
on?"

"What's one thing you can't say no to?"

"If you wrote an autobiography, what would you call
it?"

"What would your friends say is the best thing about
you?"

"What's your favorite food? The worst food?"

"If you could go anywhere in the world, where would it be?"

"If you could have any job, what would you want to do?"

"If you could be anyone but yourself, who would you want to be?"

"If you had three wishes, what would they be?"

"What's your favorite memory from growing up?"

"Tell me about your best friend."

Current Events

"Did you see the news today?"

"What do you think about the transit strike?"

"How about the Reds? You think they're going to win tonight?"

Questions make for good kindling on the small talk fire, but be sure not to make it sound like you're giving them the third degree or something. It's good to put in your own thoughts, questions, and comments about the things they're talking about. Never forget the 60–40 rule, and you should be fine.

Small Talk Questions to Avoid

- How many kids do you want?
- What time of year do you think is best for a wedding?
- Do you prefer to sleep on the right or left side of the bed?
- How would you redecorate my place?
- Do you snore?
- Can we see each other next weekend and the weekend after that?
- What do you miss about your last girlfriend/boyfriend?
- Would you get this blackhead for me?
- Are you a virgin? If not, how old were you when you lost your virginity?

Date Chatter

After the Small Talk

Researchers say 80 percent of women think that they are too fat! In one survey, women were asked what three words they would most like to hear from a guy. The most common answer was not "I love you" but "You've lost weight." Of course, save this for after the small talk. If you barely know the woman, you aren't educated enough to tell her that her weight has changed. Save it for later in the relationship.

Source: "SIRC Guide to Flirting," Kate Fox, Social Issues Research Center, n.d., http://www.sirc.org/publik/flirt.html

Finding Out More about Your Date
without Going Too Deep

So you want to know more about your date but you've learned your lesson in not sharing too much too soon. How do you do it? Here are three ways of sleuthing if the person sitting across from you is into you.

Use Humor

If every word I said could make you laugh, I'd talk forever.

—Anonymous

Okay, so you aren't exactly ever going to be a contestant on *Last Comic Standing*, but humor is still an important part of small talk. Even cheesy humor (as long as it isn't a pickup line) can help people to understand who you are and how you think. And it can lighten up the conversation so they feel free to be themselves as well. But what do you do if funny doesn't just roll off your tongue? Like everything else, humor takes practice. The best way to get your funny bone in action is to watch funny movies, read funny books, and figure out if you are a goofball or a wit master. Is your sense of humor dry or slapstick? Is it good-natured, or does it have an edge?

Just remember when using humor that just as art is in the eye of the beholder, humor is in the ear of the listener, not the mouth of the comedian.

Stupid Joke—A grasshopper walks into a bar, and the bartender shouts, "Hey, we've got a drink named after you!" So the grasshopper responds, "What? You have a drink named Bob?"

Eye Contact

Yes, even the eyes can participate in small talk. Are you receiving a long stare while the conversation is going? If you're interested, you probably love their attentiveness. Otherwise, they're just creeping you out. Likewise, if you're staring your crush down and they're not reciprocating, they're either not confident, not interested, or—you guessed it—creeped out at your staring!

The best thing to remember when someone is speaking to you is to give them your undivided attention. And that includes eye contact, but not necessarily *undivided* eye contact. You can show that you're listening intently by staring down at the table and nodding and then look up and make eye contact strategically when it's time to respond or show support of what they're saying. Mix things up a little.

Looook deep into my eyes . . . buwaah haa haa haa haa.

The best rule of thumb we can offer is keep things fresh, but when in doubt, make eye contact. It shows interest, respect, and best of all, confidence.

79

Everyday events can be great small talk. They help you figure out what you have in common, if anything. Some tips:

Pick easy topics—your day, the surroundings, non-argumentative stuff.

Memorize some questions you want to ask them.

Read the local culture newspaper and know what's going on in town.

Talk about something other than yourself unless they ask (remember, guys, women love to talk about themselves and feel like you don't like them if you only talk about yourself and don't allow them to talk).

Talk low, talk slow, and don't say too much.

—John Wayne

Date Chatter

Small Talking Up
the Family
and Friends

4

who talk about what life has taught them never fail to keep the attention of their listeners.

—Dale Carnegie

The Art of Small Talk can take some subtle turns when it goes from small talk with someone you are interested in to small talk with significant people in their life. Many a dreaded meeting with "important" people has ended in disaster at the hands of someone who doesn't understand or make the transition from their date to their date's protection network—a.k.a. *trusted inner circle*. For the most part friends, family, and coworkers often see their jobs as protectors of the hearts and minds of their loved ones. So when it comes to small talk, you have to have their goals in mind before you dive into a conversation.

Unlike the small talk you had with your date over dinner and at the movies, the extended family and friends small talk is about them getting to know *you* and not so much about you getting to know them. That's why it can feel like the first meeting is a grilling. And that's what can make the moment so excruciating. Knowing you are going to be getting the third degree from the familial review committee can be a frightening prospect, but we have some ideas that just might help you turn horror into excitement.

Meeting the Family

You feel like meeting the family can make or break you. But just to calm your nerves, it really isn't that bad. We always hope our boyfriend/girlfriend will get along famously with everyone, especially our family, but if they don't, it isn't an automatic out. So if you're scared of that first meeting, just relax. It isn't as bad as you think. But that said, it is still important because your date will be watching you to see how friendly and easy to get along with you are. Follow the general small talk guidelines. Make the conversation 50–50 as far as talking. Come prepared with ideas of things to talk about. Listen. All the basic rules apply, but there are also some differences when it comes to the family.

The biggest difference is that they are really only interested in figuring out who you are and if you are good

Ahhhh, parents. I wish there was a good book about parents.

(Shameless plug for Hayley's book *Stupid Parents*)

for their beloved Jack/Judy. They aren't really looking for you to take an interest in them and to explore who they are like you do when you are dating someone. That said, you should still take an interest in them, their home, their jobs, and their hobbies. But don't look at this as just as much an opportunity for you to grill them as it is for them to grill you. You shouldn't be the alpha dog here. Be prepared to roll over and be sniffed. Be prepared to be sincere, forthright, and congenial. You should show a genuine interest in them but more importantly in their loved one.

If they notice that your date is happier when they are with you, then you've scored major points. So don't neglect your date while trying to impress the family. Continue to small talk with them to some extent while including the family as well. The key is to appear relaxed and confident. And as we say, fake it till you make it! You don't have to *feel* confident to look confident. It can be faked. So smile, breathe, talk, and listen.

The next thing to remember is to avoid TMI. If it's important on a date, it's twice as important when meeting family and friends. You can easily embarrass your date by sharing too much information about them or your relationship, so be aware of how much it is proper to share before you go in. Ask them how much the family knows about you and what kind of relationship they have with them so you are more informed before you start to disclose. Remember, the key to small talking the family is to show them who you are and how easy you are to get along with. So avoid TMI at all costs. That spells complete disaster.

Good small talk starters for meeting the family:

- Ask your date's parents about where they work, how long, and what they do.
- If the parents are together (or your date's siblings are married), ask how they met.
- Pets! Ask about the dog that's jumping on you incessantly and if it's "an active breed."

Small Talking Friends

Friends aren't too dissimilar to family, but there are some subtle differences. Unless your date is super close to their family, you will probably find that friends are more likely to be a part of your dating life in the future. You will more than likely double date with them, spend weekends with them, and have them over to your house, so hitting it off with friends can be really important. While the family was all about getting to know you, friends are a little more 50–50. Sure, they'll want to grill you to make sure you are right for their friend, but deep down they'll also want to know if you are right for them as a new friend. That means you can spend more time questioning them, finding out what they like and what memories they have with your date, and so on.

Good small talk starters for meeting the friends:

- When did you and (date's name) meet?
- Where do you work?
- Do you have kids?
- Where are you from?

Meeting the Co-workers

The best thing you can do when it comes to meeting co-workers is do a little recon. Talk to your date about who you are going to be meeting and the kind of relationship your date has with them. Then the best rule of thumb is not to volunteer anything about the relationship beyond when and how you met, unless your date goes there. Most of the time your date just wants to show you off to co-workers. That means both physically and mentally. This is when your sense of humor can really shine, but even if you aren't the funniest person in the world, taking a genuine interest in the people you meet will score major points at work. So just like the rest of your small talking situations, show genuine interest and shoot for 50–50. Find out what interests they have outside of work. Don't talk to them about your date as much as about them and their lives. They aren't usually voters in your date's dating life; they are usually just good thermometers your date uses to see how you react to their world. In some situations, workmates are also off-workmates, and in those scenarios the conversations might resemble more of the friend or family model. But either way, a genuine interest in others will always be your best calling card.

**Small talk starters
for work functions:**

- "What are the company's biggest areas of growth?"
- "What's your history with the company?"
- "What's something that most people are surprised to hear about the company?"
- "What is the most top secret, exciting project you can tell me about without having to kill me?"

Getting the Kids on Your Side

A lot of times when people meet the family or friends for the first time, they overlook very important allies in the making: any kids present. Kids can be your biggest fans and an easy fan base to generate. Unlike the adults, they aren't cynical of your intellect or doubtful that you're good enough; they just want to know if you know how to play. So the first thing you have to do when meeting the family is look the kids in the eyes. Make sure they understand that you consider them people too. Often in these kinds of get-togethers they are overlooked. That's why when you, as someone new, notice them, you've scored an instant point. Then throughout the meeting make sure to talk to them. Ask them stupid questions if they're little, like "Why is the sky purple today?" This spawns a silly game of kid small talk. Take an interest in their hobbies if they're a little older.

When you show yourself kid-friendly, you score major points not only with the kids, who will talk about you long after you leave, but also with their parents and, more importantly, your date. Nothing is sexier than someone who likes and is good with kids. We all assume kids have an innate sense of good and evil, just like animals, and when

they like someone, we think, *Wow, they must be okay then!*
It's also just very charming to see an adult care enough to interact with the kids you love. So whatever you do, don't forget small talk with the kids of the clan! You'll score major points all around.

Hayley

Women love men who love kids! I know that for women it is such a great sign when your guy interacts with kids. The first thing you think is, *Wow, he's great with kids; he'll make an awesome dad!* And we're hooked. That might be freaky to the guys reading this, but calm down; it doesn't mean we want to go home and start making babies. It simply means you've just made a major deposit in the love bank, and we've checked off one item on the picket-fence fantasy list!

Michael

Yes, and your two children took to me pretty quickly, if my memory serves me correctly. Of course, your two "kids" had tails and a litter box.

The Doctor Dolittle of Small Talk

Now we come to the Wild Kingdom of small talk. What single person doesn't want to make sure that their most important family member, their pet, clicks with their date? It's almost pre-requisite. I mean, if she doesn't like your dog, then all bets are off. And if your cat just hisses at him and claws him, then the red flag instantly goes up. So make sure to do your best to small talk with the animals. You don't have to love them, but you can't just ignore them or, worse yet, act afraid of them. Nothing says, "Oh well, I guess he isn't the one," like a "Get away!" pointed directly at the fluffy love of her life.

Come on! Give pookums a big kiss.

Here's what you do so as not to tick off either pet or pet owner: Make sure you know before-hand what you are going into. Find out what kind of animals they have before you meet the pets. Ask the important questions: breed, size, name, where they got them. Basically, you ac-complish two things through this investigation: You prepare yourself for the ultimate meeting of the canine/feline judge, *and* you show your

94

date that you are interested in an important "person" in their life. So ask questions about their friend, and then be prepared to talk with them when you meet. Unless your date has told you otherwise, you should address the pets as soon as you see them. Get down to their level, on the floor or couch, and talk to them as if you love them. You don't have to spend hours rubbing them down or cuddling; just get through the initial meeting like a true friend. Then you can get back to your real affection—your date. But without that first interaction you're going to look like an inconsiderate clod, so take time to small talk the animals.

A Cat Story

I have two cats, and when Michael first met them, he scored major points. I told him ahead of time about their personalities. They were like kids to me, so it was important to me that he understood them. Puppy is a wild one. She loves to wrestle and play, just like a dog (hence the name). But Piglet is more subtle, a little more intuitive and picky, so I told Michael not to expect too much out of her. When Michael sat down on my couch and I started to play with Puppy on the floor, he began to talk to a cowering Piglet. Before I knew it she was on his lap, rubbing her head against his chin. At that point I knew he was a good guy. He passed the cat challenge!

Crazy Cat Woman

I knew as soon as I saw Hayley's cats that any guy could get Puppy to like him, but Piglet was the decision maker. And while I reveled in the fact that I wooed her black cat into submission, Hayley turned into a crazy cat woman, playing with Puppy by throwing her around and talking in a feline-frenzy-inducing pace and octave. I have to say that her normal nighttime routine with her cats gave me "paws." My best advice: Save some of the over-the-top pet talk or feeding them out of your mouth for the second or third date!

Meeting the family, friends, co-workers, and pets can be agony, especially if you have nothing in common. That's why practicing your small talk is so important. Let small talk come to the rescue. Where there's a will, there's a way to make even the most uncomfortable meeting a breeze—at least until your date's mom brings out her "famous" casserole.

Moving from Small
Talk to Big Talk

5

Part *of the joy of dancing is conversation. Trouble is, some men can't talk and dance at the same time.*

—Ginger Rogers

If the Art of Small Talk has served you well, then you will naturally begin to feel the pull to move from small talk to big talk. This transition can be a precarious one, however. You don't want to make the move too quickly or miss the boat and never move beyond the small stuff. Like in all things, timing is everything. So let's look at the move to the big stuff.

Talking is often like dancing. One partner leading the other across the dance floor, stepping one after the other in a fluid, graceful motion. It can be exhilarating. But not unlike in dancing, if a couple forgets who's leading and who's following, things can fall apart in the dance of small talk. Women love to talk; it's true. They bond by communication. It's part of the fabric of their being, most of the time. It's what will tell them in this stage if the man is worth continuing to see or not. But women can't take the lead in conversation as it moves from small to big talk. When they do, they run the risk of plowing over the man and taking the lead in the delicate dance of getting to know one another. A woman might feel deeply much quicker than the man and so decide to share her deepest feelings before he has—talker beware! Just like we said in the section "Miss Transparent," you have to be careful about going too deep too soon or you'll scare most guys off.

Unfortunately, this isn't just a female problem. The man can just as easily dive into big talk before the relationship is ready to go there. As the man takes the lead in the relationship by pursuing the woman, chasing her, and wooing her, he should also take the lead in the emotional dance of sharing. But that doesn't mean he should take this lead without first consulting the woman. By consulting we don't mean asking her point blank if she's ready to go deeper but rather watching her for signs that she's ready to move on to big talk. The woman should be giving you nonverbal and even small verbal cues that she's ready for more. And once the man is sure that is the case, he should be the one to take the relationship there.

Here's a good rule of thumb for moving from small talk to big talk: If your date hasn't given any hint that they are ready to move from small talk to big talk, then don't take it there. If they seem to be perfectly happy to play in the shallow end of the pool, then play there too. But as you start to get hints of their willingness to share more and more of who they are, you can begin to do the same. As people get comfortable, they will naturally start to share a deeper part of themselves. And part of the delicate dance is that each of you has to be aware of the emotional movement of the other, mirroring their movement and sharing to the same depth as the other. When one overshares or moves too quickly ahead of the other to a deeper level, it can scare the other one off. So be very aware of the emotional level to which your date is willing to go before you go there yourself. Of course, as the man leads in this dance, he will have to be ready to lead the conversation where it naturally is ready to go, and the woman will have to be willing to gently assure the man that she is ready for the next move in the dance.

Wow. I feel like I'm dancing with a star.

(That isn't Evander Holyfield.)

To talk without thinking is to shoot without aiming.

—English proverb

When we were dating, I (Hayley) wanted to say "I love you" terribly bad. I remember being in an elevator and staring at Michael as the floors whizzed by. I was grinning and squirming on my toes but afraid to say what was apparently very evident by the blush of my cheeks and gleam in my eye. But I refused to be the one to take the lead in the relationship, especially on such an important topic and moving to the next level. So I hinted around with my actions. But Michael only smiled back and played a little dumb. Not until later that night as we danced in the park by moonlight did he look at me and say, "I love you." I about melted. I had been so hungry to say it all day, but hearing it from his lips first was such a comforting and romantic experience. It gave me confidence that we could safely advance into a deeper relationship because Michael was gently leading us there.

Now, if he had said "I love you" before I had hinted around at my readiness to express myself, he would have most certainly scared me off. When a guy gets ahead of me emotionally, I feel terribly awkward and fearful of his overly emotional ways. I had a history of relationships with that type of guy, ones where I had to become the man. That's why timing is everything. Both the man and the woman have to be aware of their beautiful roles in the dance of self-expression and be prepared to act upon those roles without taking on the other person's.

Likewise, I (Michael) know that if Hayley had said "I love you" to me before I had said it, I would have felt like the chase was over and the game complete. The outcome of dating was never a game to me, but the inherent chase instinct in my Y chromosome would lead me to disinterest whenever a woman would push the emotional pace. Hayley had figured out how guys who like to lead think, and that set us up for a sweet start to our relationship.

Defining the Relationship

As a relationship progresses, several landmark moments will affect where the relationship ultimately goes. And as those landmarks approach, it helps to have an understanding of the dance of moving from small talk to deep talk. One important point in a relationship is the "define the relationship" talk. Most couples go through this in order to move on to something stronger and deeper. Trouble most often occurs when one partner goes there before the other is ready. Defining the relationship can actually kill the relationship—not because it was going to die anyway but because someone went there too early. It's like taking a soufflé out of the oven too fast (Hayley analogy). If you wait until the appropriate amount of time has passed for the soufflé to be ready, you will have a wonderful dessert, but if you pull it out too early, it will deflate into a mound of goo (Michael term) that will end up in the garbage can. That doesn't mean the soufflé was bad from the get-go; it just means it was taken out too early.

If you don't pay attention to the speed your partner is going, you may end up all by yourself.

Women tend to be the ones who want to define the relationship the most. A rare man will be dying to find out if it's exclusive or not and where things will be going over the next days and weeks before the woman. But that's not usually the case. For example, in general, a man is happier to have a casual relationship that goes on and on for months and even years than a woman is. (This generalization, of course, is excluding the nice guy.) Within a few months to a year, most women in a relationship will want to move it to something more, say, permanent. That's why stories of women who are pestering their boyfriends to marry them are so cliche. Women have an innate need to feel secure in love. And thank goodness, because without that, many a couple would never tie the knot.

But all that aside, it's important at this defining point of the relationship that the woman not take the reigns from the man and take the lead on steering the relationship. When a woman does this, more often than not the man will get scared and run, or he may give her an answer she isn't too pleased about—that the relationship is fine just where it is. See, when a woman wants to define the relationship, what she really wants is to move to the next level officially. Unfortunately, when she leads this discussion, there is a 50–50 chance that her guy won't want to go to the next level just yet. Then the woman is left with the decision whether to keep on in limbo or to say good-bye and move on to the next guy. We've seen many a young woman attempt to lead a man to move on to the next level, only to destroy the growing relationship. The solution? The best route is for the woman to allow the man to take the lead and start the "define the relationship" talk himself. Of course, this demands that the man step up and care for the relationship enough to pursue it to the next level, and not only that but also to talk with the woman about this idea. Men can't be so callous as to milk the relationship for all it's worth without ever intending to move to the next level—nor can they be too lazy to move the relationship where they know they'd like to go someday. So men need to step it up and start to initiate serious talks that move you from small talk to big talk as they sense from the woman's demeanor and their own hearts that the relationship is ready to move along. It is truly a dance and should be respected as such.

Keeping the Small Talk Alive

Once the relationship has progressed into big talk territory, don't get so enamored with the deep stuff that you forget all about the small talk. Small talk is what landed you there in the first place, so don't forget the beauty of it. It's still an essential part of flirting and connecting. A relationship that dumps the small talk and lives exclusively on big talk can end up draining one or both of the parties involved.

It's just too much strain on a relationship not to have access to the fun and challenge of small talk. So don't throw the baby out with the bathwater. Keep the small talk alive for years and years!

Hayley

I started watching a TV show called *Future Weapons* just so I could make conversation with Michael over dinner. Coming from a family with a big military background, he loves and totally understands everything about guns and ammo and stuff, and I know absolutely nothing. So I started watching, and now I can at least make a little small talk with him here and there. Even once you're married, small talk keeps things alive.

Michael

Good point. Small talk isn't just for strangers. I'll watch the occasional *Oprah* to see what John Travolta is crying about this week just so I'm in the know and we can discuss it over meat loaf. Small talk is just as important with people who are close to you! Oh, and thanks, Hayley, for learning more about weapons of mass conversation!

George is a radio announcer, and when he walks under a bridge . . . you can't hear him talk.

—Stephen Wright

Moving from Small Talk to Big Talk

The End

so much easier to pray for a bore than to go and see one.

—C. S. Lewis

Small talk isn't a luxury or just something you need to get past to get to the good stuff. It really is something that all of us should be practicing, whether we're verbose or not, whether we feel like a wallflower or the life of the party. Small talk is really about caring enough about others to get outside yourself and learn about someone else. Don't let its size fool you. Small talk can pack a big wallop in the life of someone else. It can bring a smile to the face of a stranger and warm the heart of an old friend. Small talk is an art that has been lost somewhat in modern times, but we hope that with help and over time more of us can begin to experience the simple freedom and happiness that can be found in offering a stranger a few words about nothing—words that can mean so much. If you are serious about loving others as yourself and you want to be a caring individual, then no matter

112

how hard it is, you will take the leap and dive into the Art of Small Talk with both lips. Spend time researching ways to interact with people without going too deep. Practice with all kinds of people, and even your failed attempts might make someone's day. This is really one of those wonderful acts of courage that can make a difference in the world around you.

I'm ready to dive in!

If you agree with us, then spread the news of small talk. Help your shy friends break out of their prison of shyness and begin to lovingly interact with the world around them. And help your self-centered friends break free from the prison of self and start to care for others. Share the wealth of small talk with as many people as you can, and help others gain all that you can and will gain from practicing the Art of Small Talk!

The End

Hayley DiMarco writes cutting-edge and bestselling books including *Mean Girls*, *Mean Girls All Grown Up*, *Sexy Girls*, *Technical Virgin*, *Marriable*, and *Dateable*. Her goal is to give practical answers for life's problems and to encourage readers to form stronger spiritual lives. Hayley is Chief Creative Officer and founder of Hungry Planet, an independent publishing imprint and communications company that feeds the world's appetite for truth. Hungry Planet helps organizations understand and reach the multitasking mindset, while Hungry Planet books tackle life's everyday issues with a distinctly modern spiritual voice.

Michael DiMarco has worked in publisher relations, coached volleyball at the university level, and co-hosted a relationship humor radio show called *Babble of the Sexes*. He is the CEO and Publisher of Hungry Planet, working with authors who wish to reach an increasingly postmodern culture with premodern truth. Michael is the coauthor of *Marriable*, *The Art of the First Date*, and *The Art of Rejection* with his wife, Hayley, and they live in Nashville, Tennessee.

"Feeding the World's Appetite for Truth"

What makes Hungry Planet books different?

Every Hungry Planet book attacks the senses of the reader with a post-modern mind-set (both visually and mentally) in a way unlike most books in the marketplace. Attention to every detail from physical appearance (book size, titling, cover, and interior design) to message (content and author's voice) helps Hungry Planet books connect with the more "visual" reader in ways that ordinary books can't.

With writing and packaging content for the young adult and "hip adult" markets, Hungry Planet books combine cutting-edge design with felt-need topics, all the while injecting a much-needed spiritual voice.

Why are publishers so eager to work with Hungry Planet?

Because of the innovative success and profitable track record of HP projects from the best-selling *Dateable* and *Mean Girls* to the Gold Medallion-nominated *The Dirt on Sex* (part of HP's The Dirt series). Publishers also take notice of HP founder Hayley (Morgan) DiMarco's past success in creating big ideas like the "Biblezine" concept while she was brand manager for Thomas Nelson Publishers' teen book division.

How does Hungry Planet come up with such big ideas?

Hayley and HP general manager/husband Michael DiMarco tend to create their best ideas at mealtime, which in the DiMarco household is around five times a day. Once the big idea and scope of the topic are established, the couple decides either to write the content themselves or find an up-and-coming author with a passion for the topic. HP then partners with a publisher to create the book.

How do I find out more about Hungry Planet?

Use the Web, silly—www.hungryplanet.net

Because dating's not a science

—it's an art

Rediscover the lost art of dating with practical, been there done-that advice from Hayley and Michael DiMarco.

Available at your local bookstore

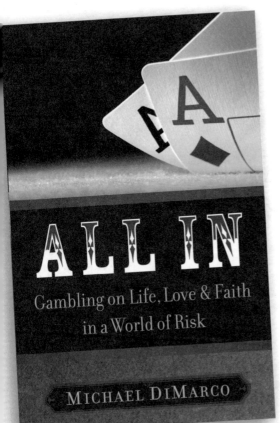

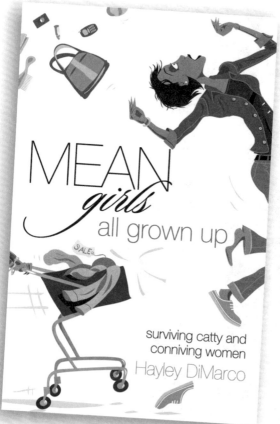